Millersburg
Crystal Glassware

By Bill Edwards

COLLECTOR BOOKS
P.O. Box 3009
Paducah, KY 42001

The current values in this book should be used only as a guide. They are not intended to set prices, which vary from one section of the country to another. Auction prices as well as dealer prices vary greatly and are affected by condition as well as demand. Neither the Author nor the Publisher assumes responsibility for any losses that might be incurred as a result of consulting this guide.

Printed by IMAGE GRAPHICS, Paducah, Kentucky

Dedication

To Mary Fair Hoffman
and
Nellie Fenton Glasgo
Who Shared So Many Memories With Me

Acknowledgements

Grateful thanks must be given in large measure to Nellie Fenton Glasgo of Canton, Ohio and Mr. Frank Fenton of Williamstown, West Virginia who shared family photos, mold drawings and old advertisements with me, as well as memories.

Thanks also to the following kind collectors who shared their glass:

Mark Boley
Don Doyle
Mrs. Frank Hazuka
Thelma Harmon
Mr. & Mrs. Paul Covert
Mr. & Mrs. Harold Wagner
Lucille Lowe
Chris Hawkins
Jack and Liz Wilson
Carl Rogers
Mr. & Mrs. Dick Shrimplin

The Millersburg Story

Interestingly enough, if John and Frank Fenton had not had such adverse personalities, there would have been no Millersburg Glass Company. Both of the brothers had come to the Martins Ferry, Ohio area in 1903 to begin a glass business in partnership.

Frank Fenton was quiet, conservative, and level headed, while brother John, eleven years older, was brash, eager, and a constant dreamer -- the pitch man of the family. Both had worked for Harry Northwood and others and each was a knowledgeable glass worker. Each wanted to make the name, Fenton, mean something in the glass business. So it began. The doer and the dreamer.

A glass decorating shop was opened in an abandoned factory they managed to rent in Martins Ferry and they began buying other companies' blanks and cutting their own designs for a ready market. While they worked, they saved and planned for their own factory.

Financial backers came, often under John's persuasive tongue; land was eventually purchased in Williamstown, West Virginia, sub-divided into lots to be sold as a money-raising venture, glass workers were sought and construction began on the Fenton Art Glass Company.

By 1907, the factory was a going concern and a prime product was iridized glass using a process Frank Fenton had originated. But in early 1908, the personalities of the Fenton brothers brought ever larger periods of friction and John decided to leave the presidency of the company, sell his interests, and go in search of his dreams. He had long felt he was being held back and that his ideas would prove he could succeed on his own, despite the hazards of the glass industry. He was thirty-eight years old, a huge strapping man with a shock of healthy brown hair and a pair of steely eyes that could almost hypnotize. He would sire five children in all.

After several weeks of travel and inquiry, John Fenton came to Holmes County, Ohio, and was immediately impressed with the countryside and the people. Here were heartland Americans, whose ancestors came from Germany and Switzerland. Also, there were the Amish, hard working farmers and businessmen whose religion required them to persue a simple way of life. John Fenton felt at ease here.

The word was spread that John Fenton felt the Millersburg area was a good one for a glass factory site and in the middle of July in 1908, a town meeting was held to discuss the possibility. Those present were excited about the prospect and a group of area people approached John Fenton with a location proposal.

By using what capitol he had from the sale of his Williamstown interests and what he could pry loose from members of his family and what he could borrow, John Fenton was able to secure by option a 54.7 acre parcel of land on the north edge of Millersburg from a group of businessmen consisting of Harvey Close, A.C. Fry, and Samuel B. Fair (who was to become much a part of the Fenton history). Just as he had done in the Williamstown venture, lots were platted and sold to gain additional capital.

On September 14, 1908, ground was broken for the factory and like John Fenton's dreams, it was to be the grandest glass plant ever. The main building was a magnificent structure, 300 by 100 feet, spanned by steel framework with no center support and featuring a well-planned work area. In addition, an adjoining building 50 by 300 feet was built to be used as a packing and shipping room, a cooper shop for producing packing barrels, and a tool shop.

The main building housed a 14-pot furnace, centrally located, with a brick stack 125 feet high and 28 feet in diameter at its base. Besides housing the work area, this building contained a mix room, a lehr area, an office and a display area for the samples of glassware for current production. (As a small girl, Mary Fair Hoffman recalls visiting the plant and this display area to chose "whatever she liked". Mrs. Hoffman, now in her 80's didn't really care for *any* of the glass but often took a piece or two just to please her father, Sam Fair).

While the construction continued, John Fenton drilled gas wells to supply a source of power and in all, eighteen wells were finally drilled. At the same time, stocks at $100.00 per share, totaling $125,000.00 were issued. Upon incorporation, those officially listed were: John Fenton, President; H.W. Stanley, Vice-President and Treasurer; Robert Fenton, Secretary; and H.F. Weber, General Sales Manager.

Finally on May 20, 1909, the first glass was poured. The initial molds were designed by Mr. Fenton and were Ohio Star and Hobstar and Feather patterns. These were not the first molds he had designed. Nellie Fenton Glasgo recalls her father personally designed a bowl featuring the profile of her mother (apparently this is the Goddess of Harvest pattern made at the Fenton's Williamstown factory).

The glass was of top quality crystal and to celebrate, open house was held the following weekend, when samples of the new product were given to all visitors. These gifts were reported to be Ohio Star handled toothpick holders in crystal.

In addition to the crystal glass, iridized glass went into production the first month using the original Fenton process. The first colors were amethyst and green, with a soft marigold added to the line a short time later. About this time a third pattern was put into production and was to be known as Millersburg Cherry. It soon became one of the "leaders" and the shapes available were increased until most useful ones were produced. John Fenton so liked this pattern that he tried several varients in design, finally arriving at the Multi-Fruits and Flowers pattern as the produced spin-off pattern.

Early shapes at Millersburg were primarily useful ones such as water sets, table pieces consisting of covered butter dishes, sugar bowls, creamers, spooners, cracker jars, toothpick holders, syrups, cruets, bowls, salt shakers, and an ale glass.

In addition, two large punch sets in both of the original patterns were produced and a beautiful footed rose bowl in Hobstar and Feather design appeared in both crystal and iridized glass.

Early in January, 1910, the celebrated line of iridized glass known as "radium" was born. This featured a softer shade of base glass color with a watery, mirror-like luster. Noted glassworker, Oliver Phillips, is credited with the process technique. The radium finish was unveiled at a Pittsburgh glass showing later that year and drew instant attention, with examples of the newly designed Big Fish and Nesting Swan patterns, as well as the three original patterns.

Following the success of the Pittsburgh show, it was decided the line should be expanded and additional molds were ordered from the Hipkins Novelty Mold Company of Martins Ferry.

In June, 1910, the well-known Courthouse bowl was produced as a gesture of appreciation to those who had laid the gas lines from the wells to the factory. These bowls, made in lettered, unlettered, radium finish and satin finish, were given away at the factory (still other examples of John Fenton's enormous generosity are the People's Vase which was designed as a tribute to the Amish and the Ohio Star punch sets, which were given to the churches and social organizations of Holmes County).

During this period the Millersburg plant was at its zenith and both radium glass and crystal were being produced. Peacocks were in vogue as a design element and John Fenton, it is said, not wanting to be outdone, bought several live Peacocks, and turned them loose on the factory grounds, so that the designers could produce a realistic design. It must have worked, for the Millersburg Peacock is the most detailed and beautiful in all of Carnival glass. But area residents were said to be less than happy with the noise these beautiful birds caused, especially during the evening hours.

Mr. Fenton and his family were involved not only in the glass factory, but always tried to enter into the community's activities as well. At one time during an annual fall festival, the Fentons provided an elaborate float wagon for the parade. Heavily decorated with bunting, the float held banquet size Ohio Star punch bowls, from which young ladies in costume passed out samples of punch to the crowd. All went well until it was learned John Fenton had spiked the punch! The town's leaders did not take kindly to this and promptly told Mr. Fenton so. While apologies were given, it was some time before the incident was forgiven.

About this time, Robert Fenton, secretary of the corporation, left the Millersburg plant and returned to his old job with the railroad at Marion, Ohio (this was not a permanent move and Robert eventually moved to Williamstown and began a career with the Fenton factory).

Rumors of financial problems had already begun to circulate, but John Fenton resisted every hint of trouble and set about to dispell any doubt by offering new patterns from the Hipkins Company. These included such patterns as Blackberry, Grape and Strawberry Wreaths; Peacock Tail Vt., Multi-Fruits and Flowers, Pipe Humidor, Potpourri, Country Kitchen and Poppy. Most were, of course, radium patterns, but Potpourri and Country Kitchen were produced in crystal in a large array of shapes including compotes, bowls, plates, berry sets, and a beautiful stemmed cake plate. An early 1911 ad shows three varieties of berry wreath bowls and a Peacock Tail varient in a very pleasing radium glass display.

In late March of 1911, the handwriting was at last on the wall and the Hipkins Company found itself forced to file suit for overdue payment of the account, including eighteen months of unpaid mold work bills. With this action, the flood gates were opened and additional lawsuits were filed by other creditors. John Fenton tried to weather it all and kept production going, but he must have known his efforts were pointless. In June of that year, the Millersburg Company was declared bankrupt and doors were closed.

But somehow, John never gave in to this truth, and tried to interest anyone who might have capital to invest in a return of the business. In October, Samuel Fair bought the plant at public sale for a price of slightly more than $14,000.00. Mr. Fair realized he was a novice in glass making but he was a businessman (and part time politician) and decided the plant was worth saving. He retained John Fenton as vice-president and consultant and was joined by John Moritz as shop manager, C.J. Fisher as secretary, M. Legillon as treasurer, and H. Kimble as foreman. The factory name was changed to the Radium Glass Company and the policy was to produce only radium glass. Production officially began in November, 1911.

For several months, Mr. Fair continued to operate, however, the bad name the bankruptcy had brought, the always keen competition and the lack of knowledge in the glass field required failure ultimately. Earlier, John Fenton had been dismissed (according to Mary Fair Hoffman, there were discrepencies in the account ledgers, however, no charges were ever brought and we can only speculate on the reasons for John Fenton's departure). In late May, the final shipment of glass left the factory to the Woolworth Company and instructions were given for workers to fill no more orders, although large amounts of finished glass remained on hand. The doors were simply closed for the second time.

Samuel Fair, like many investors, in the initial venture, lost most of his worldly assets in the closing and his daughter vividly recalls long lean times after that. She credits her mother's many strenghths with their survival as a family unit.

As for John Fenton and his family, times surely were just as painful. He drifted from one temporary job to another, still reaching for that one big chance to grab his own rainbow. He traveled as a jobber, sold advertising, always it seemed, one step ahead of his creditors, often living in hotels and occasionally leaving these with unpaid room bills. In 1918, Grace Fenton, one of the three daughters, passed away and three years later, John Fenton's wife was killed in a tragic motor accident. As a passenger in an open touring car, she was swept out onto the road when the car swerved to avoid an on-coming truck, ironically driven by Samuel Fair's son.

Survived by only two of the five original children (two had died in infancy), John Fenton passed away in January, 1934. His daughters, Mrs. Helen Fenton Elliot, and Mrs. Nellie Fenton Glasgo still reside in the eastern Ohio area. While much bitterness remained in the Millersburg area concerning John Fenton's failure as a handler of the area stock-holder's monies, no one can deny he gave us a wonderful and long lasting treasure that is Millersburg glass.

After more than a year in idleness, the factory was sold to Frank Sinclair in October, 1913. Sinclair was the organizer of the Jefferson Glass Company and once again glass production in Millersburg began. This time, however, it was to be glass for lanterns, railroad signal lights, and auto reflectors.

Many of the Millersburg molds had been transferred with the ownership of the factory and most of these were sold for scrap metal; however a few survived and were deemed suitable for production of crystal glass once again. These were shipped to the Jefferson factory in Canada and once again Millersburg patterns were put into production. These included Hobstar and Feather, Ohio Star, and Millersburg Flute designs in useful shapes including berry sets, table sets, water sets, assortments of bowls, celery trays, pickle dishes and punch sets. All of these are shown in 1915 Jefferson ads and apparently were quite popular with Canadians.

In addition, the lamp molds used for the Wild Rose and Ladies Medallion lamps

8

were sold to Riverside where they were re-tooled for use. Riverside added their name to the molds, put a *new* Wild Rose design on the interior and produced the lamps in crystal and goofus for some time.

Production at the Millersburg plant itself was again brief, and in 1919, the plant was closed and sold to the Forrester Tire and Rubber Company. The great stack was dismantled and the glassmaking equipment sold. Since that time various owners have spent brief periods in residence and a parking lot has been added in front of the factory.

But as long as the glass collectors and lovers of beauty realize the worth of Millersburg glass, the present purpose of the factory will matter little, for it has served its purpose and its place in history is assured. The people in the Millersburg area can be justly proud of their part in John Fenton's glorious dream.

Millersburg Glass Company Stock Certificate dated 1910. Courtesy Jack Wilson, Chicago, Illinois.

Post card of the Mixing Room at Millersburg Glass Company. From author's collection.

A photo of the punch wagon that John Fenton provided during a community fall festival. Punch was served from the Ohio Star punch bowls. Photo courtesy of Nellie Fenton Glasgo of Wooster, Ohio and Don Doyle of Rockford, Illinois.

Known Millersburg Crystal Patterns and Shapes

Cactus
1. Bowl-8½"-Rare

Country Kitchen
1. Advertising bowl-9"-Rare
2. Advertising plate-10"-Rare
3. Bowls (plain)-5", 9"
4. Plate (plain)-5", 7", 10", 12"
5. Table set-Rare

Cut Cosmos (Questionable)
1. Water set-Rare

Diamonds
1. Banana bowl-11"-Rare
2. Bowls-10"
3. Compote (large)-Rare
4. Table set-Rare
5. Water set

Feather and Heart
1. Water set

Hobstar Fancy (Questionable)
1. Small footed rose bowl

Hobstar and Feather
1. Applesauce boat
2. Banana plate-3 sizes
3. Banana sauces-6"
4. Berry set-5", 9"
5. Bridge set-6" (approx.)
6. Card tray-6"
7. Celery boat-10"
8. Compote
9. Cracker jar-covered-Rare
10. Ice cream set
11. Lemonade set-Rare
12. Master boat-11"
13. Nut bowl
14. Pickle dish-3 sizes
15. Plate-3 sizes-Rare
16. Punch set-Rare
17. Rose bowl-giant
18. Rose bowl whimsey-Rare
19. Sherbet
20. Spittoon whimsey-Rare
21. Squat pitcher-Rare
22. Stemmed rose bowl
23. Table set
24. Water set-Rare

Marilyn
1. Water set

Ohio Star
1. Banana bowls-3 sizes
2. Berry set-5", 9"
3. Champagne goblet-Rare
4. Cider set-Rare
5. Compote-2 varities
6. Cookie jar-Rare
7. Cruet-Rare
8. Mint dish
9. Plate-3 sizes-Rare
10. Punch set-Rare
11. Rose bowl-flat-Rare
12. Rose bowl-stemmed
13. Salt and pepper-2 sizes-Rare
14. Sherbets
15. Square bowls-5", 7", 9"
16. Square flat dishes-5", 7", 9"
17. Syrup-Rare
18. Table set-Rare
19. Toothpick holder
20. Tray whimsey-3 sizes
21. Vase
22. Vase whimsey
23. Water bottle
24. Water set-Rare
25. Wine

Palm Wreath (Questionable)
1. Bowl-6", 10"-Rare
2. Goblet
3. Table set

Potpourri
1. Cake plate, stemmed-Rare
2. Compote-2 shapes
3. Milk pitcher
4. Salver
5. Water set

Queen's Lamp
1. Oil lamp and shade-Rare

Trefoil Fine Cut
1. Bowl-9"-Rare

Wild Rose Lamp
1. Medallion lamp (no roses)-Rare

Cactus

Here's the reverse pattern normally found on Rays and Ribbons iridized bowls. In Crystal it is a very difficult item to find. Found only on the large berry bowl shape, Cactus is a well-balanced, imaginative pattern.

$85.00 (rare)   Hawkins Collection

Country Kitchen Advertising Bowl

Obviously the bowl and plate were from the same mold and both are enhanced by the rare advertising.

The bowl shown is lettered:

"Compliments of
Illinois Furniture Co.
Honest Values
3609 N. Halsted St."

$115.00 (rare)   Doyle Collection

Country Kitchen Advertising Plate

The beauty of the Country Kitchen pattern became very obvious in the plate shape and in the example shown, the rarity of added advertising is present.

It reads, "Compliments of Bijou Theatre".

The plate is flat based and measures about 10″ in diameter. The design is exterior and the plate's edges are fluted.

$125.00 (rare)   Doyle Collection

Country Kitchen Bowl (Plain)

While these berry sets are normally round or ruffled, grotesque shapes have turned up with the edges pulled into tall square-cornered shapes.

The design is all exterior and both 5″ and 9″ bowls are known.

$20.00 (5″)   Wagner Collection
$40.00 (9″)

Country Kitchen Plate (Plain)

Four sizes have been reported in this plate shape (5″, 7″, 10″, 12″) and of course all are flat based.

The design shows to its best advantages in this shape and really establishes the beauty of the design.

$75.00 (average)   Wagner Collection

Country Kitchen Table Set

Like other table sets, the Country Kitchen had a covered butter dish, a spooner, a covered sugar and a creamer. Each piece was artistic and well designed. Shown is a part of the set, the creamer.

$200.00 (complete)   Lowe Collection

Country Kitchen Varient (Opal)

The word rare is easily used, but here is a bowl that couldn't be called anything else!

As you can see it is a varient of the Country Kitchen bowl with an *opalescent edge*! I know of no other example in any pattern in Millersburg opalescent and I'm very honored to show it. It measures 7½" wide and is 2¾" deep. Two examples are reported.

$500.00 (very rare)   Rogers Collection

Cut Cosmos Tumbler

As I said in my Millersburg Carnival book, I really feel this could be a pattern from the Ohio Company, but no proof exists. Only time will tell.

The glass is clear and sparkling and the mold work very fine.

Pitcher (rare), $125.00   Covert Collection
Tumbler (rare), $35.00

Diamonds Banana Boat

Rare indeed is this beauty! It is pulled into the banana boat shape from a bowl shape and measures about 11″ in length. The odd thing is, the bowls are very elusive and this is the only example we've seen of the banana boat.

$150.00   Covert Collection

Diamonds Compote

Here is one of the larger compotes from Millersburg and what a rare and beautiful one it is! The top has curved scallops formed by the diamond rings below; the pattern is repeated around the base. It stands 12¼" tall and has a bowl diameter of 10¼".

$300.00 (rare)   Covert Collection

Diamonds Table Set

   While we show only the covered butter dish, obviously the entire set exists. Some of the diamonds have a ruby flash. Tumblers in this pattern have also been reported with this process. This is a rare pattern and shape.

$300.00 (Butter dish only)   Doyle Collection
                                          (from Lowe Collection)

Feather and Heart Water Set

Mostly seen in Carnival glass where it is quite scarce, this nicely patterned near-cut design is rare in crystal.

The mold work is very crisp and the glass typically sparkling like most Millersburg.

Pitcher (rare), $150.00   Wilson Collection
Tumbler (rare), $35.00

Hobstar Fancy Rosebowl (Stemmed)

Perhaps this little cutie isn't Millersburg, but it certainly has all the qualities to be. The design is crisp and imaginative, the glass clear and sparkling, and mold work top-notch.

It stands 4¾" tall on a scalloped base and measures 4½" across the widest area of the bowl.

$50.00 (scarce)   Covert Collection

Hobstar and Feather Applesauce Boat

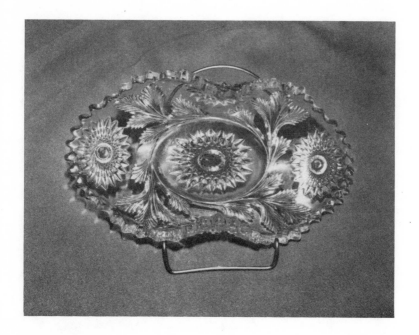

Shaped much like the larger banana dish, this applesauce boat measures 4″ x 8″. The feathers can be found both clear and frosted.

$85.00   Hawkins Collection

Hobstar and Feather Banana Bowl

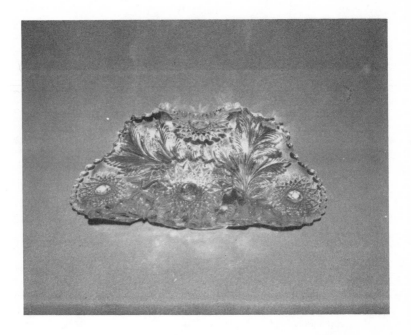

Almost too pulled out to be a beautiful shape, this whimsey has its unique features. It is large, some 11″ in length. The turned up area is quite high and somewhat irregular, but these are rare.

$150.00 (rare)   Wagner Collection

Hobstar and Feather Berry Set

Both large and small bowls were grouped to form this very lovely berry set, but for identification purposes we show only the 6″ bowl. Notice the hobstar's center is prismatic.

Large bowl, $50.00   Wagner Collection
Small bowl, $28.00

Hobstar and Feather Bridge Set

Shown is the complete set made up of spade, club, heart, and diamond shaped mint dishes.

The diamond one measures 5¾″ x 5″. It has one center hobstar with the feathers swirling around the body.

Interestingly enough, the diamond and heart shapes are also found in marigold Carnival glass where they are very rare. Occasionally the edges are gilted on the crystal pieces.

$50.00 each (rare)   Wagner Collection

Hobstar and Feather Celery Boat

A close comparison of this piece with the photo of the Hobstar and Feather pickle dish will show the obvious differences. This beautiful boat shape measures 10″ in length, 4¾″ across the top and 2½″ deep at the center. The glass is, again, thick and heavy and quite sparkling.

$80.00 (scarce)   Harmon Collection

Hobstar and Feather Compote

The same mold was used for this item as the footed rosebowl shown in this pattern. It stands 5¼″ tall and has a rim diameter of 5½″-6″, depending on the shaping. It is a very beautiful compote, as you can see.

$75.00 (scarce)   Author's Collection

Hobstar and Feather Cracker Jar

Also from the 1910 line, this beautiful covered cracker jar or cookie jar more than lives up to the rest of the shapes in this pattern. It is scarce and much sought after.

$250.00 (rare)   Wagner Collection

Hobstar and Feather Giant Rosebowl

Just like the iridized ones, this giant rosebowl is a sight to behold. Standing 9″ tall with a 7¼″ diameter, the glass is very heavy and massive, but extremely graceful.

$400.00 (rare)   Wagner Collection

Hobstar and Feather Giant Whimsey

Pulled from the giant rosebowl shape, this beautiful compote whimsey is simply spectacular.

To date I've heard of only this one, but certainly others
may exist. This was photographed in a Millersburg festival
display.

$500.00 (rare)   Private Collection

Hobstar and Feather Ice Cream Set

Both the large and small bowls making up this set are shaped the same and have the typically round configuration without ruffling that constitutes the ice cream bowl shape.

Found in both clear and frosted, this set is made up of a master bowl and six smaller ones.

$300.00 Set (scarce)   Wagner Collection

Hobstar and Feather Mammoth Pitcher

What a beauty this is! It is shown in a 1910 Butler Brothers catalog as a "mammoth" pitcher (the price 35 cents!).

It is 8″ tall with a girth of 22½″! It holds 3½ quarts of liquid.

Needless to say, it is a rare and very desirable showpiece.

$950.00 (rare)   Covert Collection

Hobstar and Feather Nut Bowl

While this shape lends itself to several uses, the general use was to hold nuts or mints. It measures 5 7/8″ x 4¼″ and the feathers are frosted; however it can also be found with unfrosted feathers.

$50.00   Hawkins Collection

Hobstar and Feather Pickle Dish

I've heard this called a celery dish but it really isn't that large.

Measuring 7½ " x 5 ", the pickle dish has a deep saw tooth edge and is of very thick glass. The Hobstars have a button center and the pickle dish is found in both clear and frosted.

There are at least 3 sizes in this shape.

$40.00   Author's Collection

Hobstar and Feather Plate

What could possibly show off this artistic pattern better than this fluted edge plate? It was flattened from the bowl shape and is, of course, much scarcer. It measures 11″ across.

$125.00 (rare)   Hawkins Collection

Hobstar and Feather Punch Set

Here is my favorite punch set in Carnival glass and certainly it must rank high on anyone's list in crystal. It is a massive item, and very symmetrical.

Found in both plain and with frosted feathers, it was made both at Millersburg and later at Jefferson Glass in Canada.

$1,500.00 Complete   Shrimplin Collection

Hobstar and Feather Sherbet

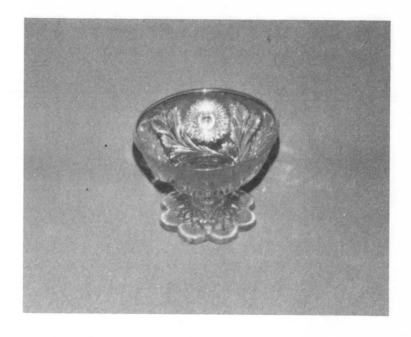

Even for a very massive design, this stemmed sherbet has a dainty look to it. While they aren't as rare as some shapes in this pattern in crystal, a *very rare* iridized marigold one has turned up. They stand 4″ tall and have a 3 7/8″ diameter.

$28.00   Wagner Collection

Hobstar and Feather Spittoon Whimsey

This beauty was fashioned from the standard water tumbler and is a rare item indeed. Please note the feathers are not frosted and the hobstar's center button is plain rather than prismatic. The spittoon whimsey is 3½" in diameter and 2 7/8" tall. No others have been reported.

$500.00 (rare)

Boley Collection
Photo courtesy of
Mark Boley Studios, Millersburg, Ohio

Hobstar and Feather Stemmed Rosebowl

Shaped from the stemmed compote, this beautiful rosebowl is 5¾" tall and measures 3¾" across the top. It has four mold lines and the base has a very beautiful hobstar like the one on the base of the giant rosebowl. The stem is fluted.

$100.00 (rare)   Harmon Collection

Hobstar and Feather Table Set

Shown are three parts of the four piece set. Only the covered butter dish is missing. Again, the glass is heavy and brilliant, giving a massive look. All pieces are rare, but not nearly as rare as the iridized ones.

$500.00 Complete (rare)   Wagner Collection

Hobstar and Feather Tankard Water Set

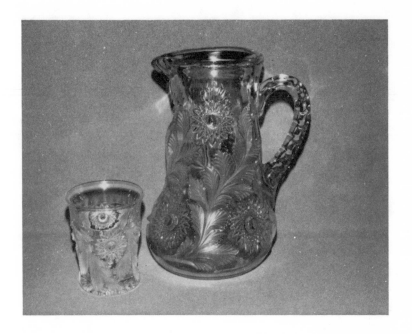

Found more often than the squat water pitcher, the tankard shown measures 9¼″ tall. The glass is thick and sparkling and the base shows a pontil mark. Both plain and frosted feathers are known and I've seen one pitcher with a highly ornamented metal lip.

The tumbler measures 3¾″ tall and is belled. It has a large hobstar in the base.

Pitcher (rare), $200.00   Harmon Collection
Tumbler (rare), $85.00 each

Hobstar and Feather Whimsey Tray

Obviously pulled from a flat piece, all four sides have been pulled straight up to form a shallow tray. Several sizes are known, but the one shown is about 7″ in diameter.

$100.00 (rare)   Wagner Collection

Marilyn Water Set

Perhaps this is Millersburg's best near cut water set and while hard to find in iridized glass, the crystal version is seldom seen, with tumblers harder to locate than the pitcher. The glass is, of course, quite heavy.

Pitcher, $155.00   Wilson Collection
Tumbler, $30.00

Ohio Star Berry Bowl

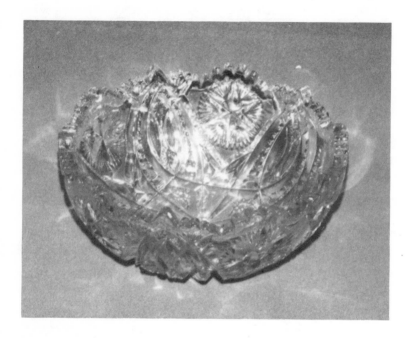

Just like most berry sets, this one has a master bowl and six smaller ones. The glass is quite thick and the mold work excellent. Shapes may vary greatly but most are simply round.

$300.00 set   Wagner Collection

Ohio Star Card Tray Whimsey

Shown in a 1910 Butler Brothers Catalog, this oval card tray measures 4¼" in length and 3½" across. It rolls slightly upward from the base. It is rare. It has been reported in a larger size also.

$95.00 (rare)   Covert Collection

Ohio Star Celery Tray

Perhaps not as graceful as some Millersburg shapes, this 9″ long celery tray isn't one you'd soon forget. It has a gentle curve on each side from the flat base and does manage to show off the design.

$100.00 (rare)   Wagner Collection

Ohio Star Cider Set

The massive look of this cider set is deceptive. The pitcher is only 10″ tall and the gently belled glass is about ½″ taller than the regular tumbler. All in all, a rare and graceful set that has a tankard appeal.

Pitcher (rare), $375.00
Tumbler (rare), $85.00

Doyle Collection

Ohio Star Compote (Short)

Ohio Star Compote (Short)

Here's the compote shape of this pattern often pulled into a rosebowl and as we said, it is a little beauty. It measures 4¾″ tall and 5¼″ across.

$250.00 (scarce)   Wagner Collection

Ohio Star Compote (Tall)

This tall compote (7″) is usually found in Carnival glass where only four examples are known, so you know how rare the crystal version is.

The stem is heavy, solid glass and the base exterior has the Ohio Star design.

$300.00 (rare)   Doyle Collection

Ohio Star Cruet

If you like cruets, you'll love this cutie. It is 5¾″ tall and I've seen two different stoppers, but I believe the one shown is the original. It is very hard to find and is a show-stopper.

$200.00 (rare)   Wagner Collection

Ohio Star Flat Mint Dish

Almost square, this 5¼ ″ dish has only a slight turn-up on the edges. It too, dates from 1910 and sold at wholesale price for 3½ cents! Today this rarity would grace any fine collection of crystal.

$85.00 (rare)   Wagner Collection

Ohio Star Plate (Round)

The round 6¾" plate shown is from the sauce dish and has been flattened out. It is a rare one and why more weren't made is a mystery, considering its beauty.

$250.00   Lowe Collection

Ohio Star Punch Set

Here is the master punch set John Fenton used on his "infamous" festival float and it is indeed both massive and impressive. I rank it with the very best sets in pressed glass and the price supports that. Five sets have been reported to date, but surely there are others.

Complete (rare)   Wilson Collection
$1,600.00

Ohio Star Rosebowl (Large)

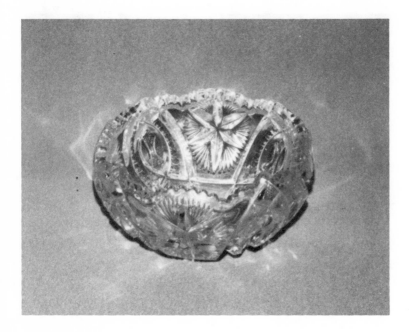

Pulled in from the large heavy bowl shape, this large flat rosebowl measures about 7″ across. Its scalloped edges give an interesting look and of course, the brilliance of the glass speaks quality.

$185.00 (scarce)   Wagner Collection

Ohio Star Shakers (Squat)

Just why two types of shakers were designed in one pattern is indeed a mystery, but these, like their cousins are very rare.

I know of two sets of these squat shakers.

$500.00 Pair (rare)   Lowe Collection

Ohio Star Shakers (Tall)

Rare isn't the word for these beautiful salt and pepper shakers. Measuring about 1½″ taller than the squat shaker, these are the only reported examples in this shape.

$500.00 Pair (rare)   Covert Collection

Ohio Star Square Bowl

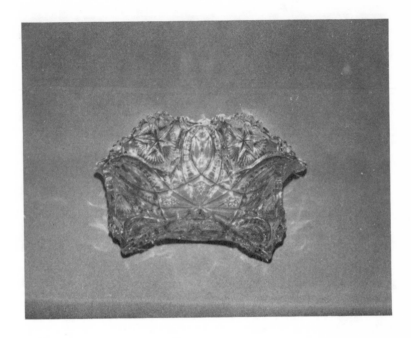

If you'll compare this square bowl with the square dish in this pattern, you'll see the distinction. The bowl is much deeper and has a gentle ruffling to the sides. While rare, it is more easily found than the square dish.

$150.00 (rare)   Wagner Collection

Ohio Star Square Dish

Again, these are found in several sizes including 5", 7", and 9". The one shown measures just over 9" and is certainly a beautifully shaped low dish.

$285.00 (rare)   Wagner Collection

Ohio Star Stemmed Rosebowl

Here is the standard 5¼" stemmed compote turned in to form a rosebowl. I've seen one with the top almost entirely closed off, but they'll vary greatly. They are, needless to say, on the rare side and very attractive.

$300.00 (scarce)   Wagner Collection

Ohio Star Syrup

Here is a charmer that anyone who likes crystal would adore and it is a rare item indeed. Only the one has been reported so far.

It stands 5¼″ tall and has a heavy silvered metal spout. Note that the notched handle is like that on the toothpick holder.

$900.00

Lowe Collection
Photo courtesy Lucille Lowe,
Killbuck, Ohio

Ohio Star Table Set

Oh, what a beautiful sight this complete set makes and the butter dish has the only base without damage I've encountered.

Each piece is a treasure and all together the set is spectacular.

$500.00 Set (rare)   Wagner Collection

Ohio Star Water Bottle

Water bottles have a charm all their own and the Ohio Star is one of the best. The design covers most of the available space and even the spoke-and-notch design on the neck adds interest. It is 8¾″ tall.

$275.00 (rare)   Doyle Collection

Ohio Star Water Set

Here is the standard water set and a comparison with the cider set shown in this pattern will evidence many differences. It is of very heavy glass and is a desirable set to own, but slightly less rare than the other set.

Pitcher (rare), $300.00   Wagner Collection
Tumbler (each), $55.00

Ohio Star Whimsey Lamp

While I can't verify the origin of this lamp, other than the component parts *are* Millersburg, it shows what a little time and imagination can create.

The body of the lamp is an Ohio Star water bottle while the shade is a large berry bowl in the same pattern, turned upside down.

I doubt if it was ever a production item but *may* have been a worker's project.

$900.00

Lowe Collection
Photo courtesy of Lucille Lowe,
Killbuck, Ohio

Ohio Star Wine

What a joy these small wines are! The all-over design, the clear sparkling glass, and the balanced design make them treasures in miniature. They are highly sought, especially by collectors of miniature glass pieces.

$35.00 each (rare)   Covert Collection

Palm Wreath Bowl

While I list this as a questionable Millersburg pattern, I'm fairly confident it is. At the center of the giant hobstar is an Ohio Star. This is surrounded by very beautiful wreathes of palm-like leaves. The bowl shown is 9½" in diameter and 4¼" deep. Surely other shapes exist, but haven't been reported at this time.

$250.00 (rare)   Covert Collection

Palm Wreath Creamer

Perhaps this is one half of a breakfast set or part of a table set. It is the same pattern as the bowl and is a very scarce item.

The Millersburg attribution is a questionable one, but the glass and mold work are compatible.

$60.00 (rare)   Covert Collection

Palm Wreath Goblet

Like the bowl and creamer also shown in this pattern, the glass and design quality are much like most Millersburg products.

Needless to say, these are quite hard to locate.

$60.00 each (rare)   Covert Collection

Potpourri Compote

    Shown is one of *three* shapes from the same mold. Besides the compote shape, a stemmed salver and cake plate are known.

    The Potpourri compote stands 7″ tall and is roughly 8″ across the bowl. The example shown has straight sides.

$100.00 (scarce)   Author's Collection

Potpourri Salver (Footed)

Here is the flattened compote called a salver. It is more common than the straight sided compote shape but none-the-less is an impressive piece of glass. It was used to hold slices of cake.

$85.00 (scarce)   Doyle Collection

Potpourri Stemmed Cake Plate

Shown is the only example of a completely flat stemmed cakeplate I've encountered. It was shaped from the salver shape and it is quite rare.

$275.00 (rare)   Covert Collection

Queen's Lamp

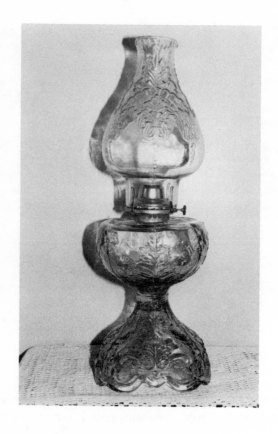

While the Millersburg origin may be somewhat questionable, I'm sure enough to list this very rare lamp here. Please note the chimney *matches* the lamp's body -- a most unusual happening in table lamps. Two green iridized ones are known but this is the first reported in crystal.

$750.00 (rare)   Hazuka Collection

Trefoil Fine Cut Bowl

    If this pattern looks familiar, it should, for it is the exterior pattern of the Carnival glass Many Stars bowls.

    In crystal it is quite rare with only two or three examples reported.

$250.00 (rare)   Covert Collection

Wild Rose Lamp (Riverside)

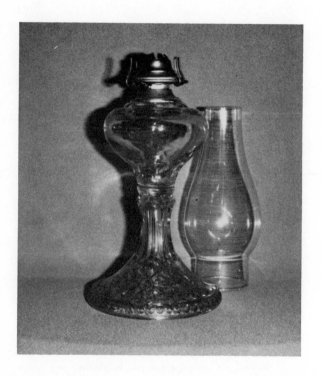

Two sizes are reported in the crystal Wild Rose lamp. The smaller size, shown, measures 8½″ to the top of the font and has a base diameter of 5½″.

The design is interior, much more artistic than the iridized counterpart which has an exterior design, and the example shown has traces of a "goofus" finish.

As I said earlier, this is *not* a Millersburg product but was produced from a re-tooled Millersburg mold. It is marked "RIVERSIDE CLINCH ON COLLAR".

$75.00 (scarce)   Author's Collection

Other popularly priced illustrated value guides from COLLECTOR BOOKS:

Barbie Dolls by Paris, Susan & Carol Manos, 5½ x 8½, 80 pages, paperbound, $5.95.

The Basket Book by Don & Carol Raycraft, 5½ x 8½, 80 pages, paperbound, $5.95.

Black Glass by Margaret James, 5½ x 8½, 80 pages, paperbound, $5.95.

Coffee Mills by Terry Friend, 5½ x 8½, 80 pages, paperbound, $5.95

Decorated Country Stoneware by Don & Carol Raycraft, 5½ x 8½, 80 pages, paperbound, $5.95.

Metal Molds by Eleanore Bunn, 5½ x 8½, 80 pages, paperbound, $5.95.

The Oak Book by Jane Fryberger, 5½ x 8½, 80 pages, paperbound, $5.95.

Police Relics by George Virgines, 5½ x 8½, 80 pages, paperbound, $5.95.

Sea Shells by Carol Glassmire, 5½ x 8½, 80 pages, paperbound, $5.95.

Trolls by Susan Miller, 5½ x 8½, 80 pages, paperbound, $5.95.

The Wicker Book by Jane Fryberger, 5½ x 8½, 80 pages, paperbound, $5.95.

Order from your favorite bookstore or
COLLECTOR BOOKS
P.O. Box 3009
Paducah, KY 42001

When ordering, please add $1.00 for postage and handling.

Write for free listing of all other COLLECTOR BOOK titles.